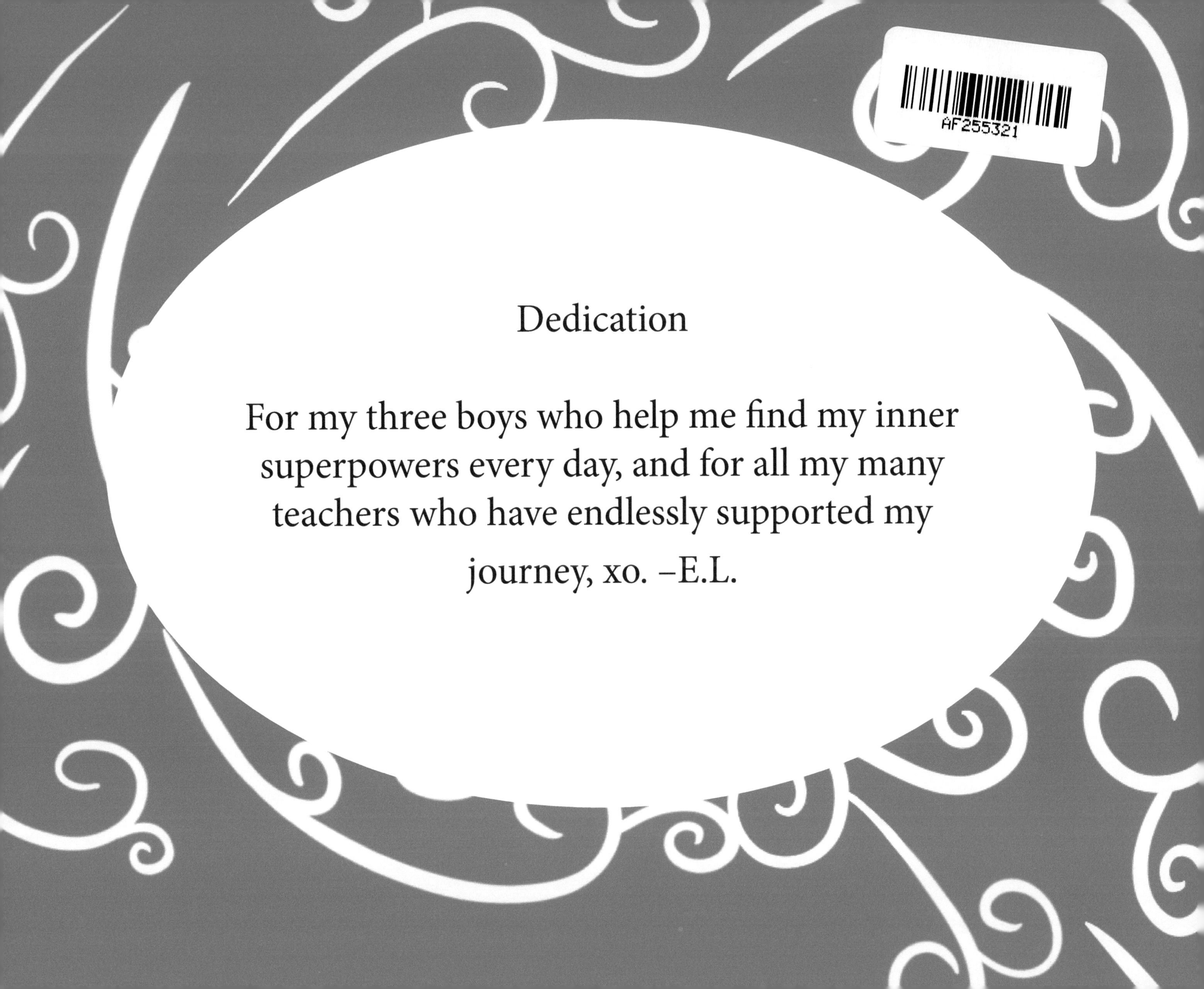

Dedication

For my three boys who help me find my inner superpowers every day, and for all my many teachers who have endlessly supported my journey, xo. –E.L.

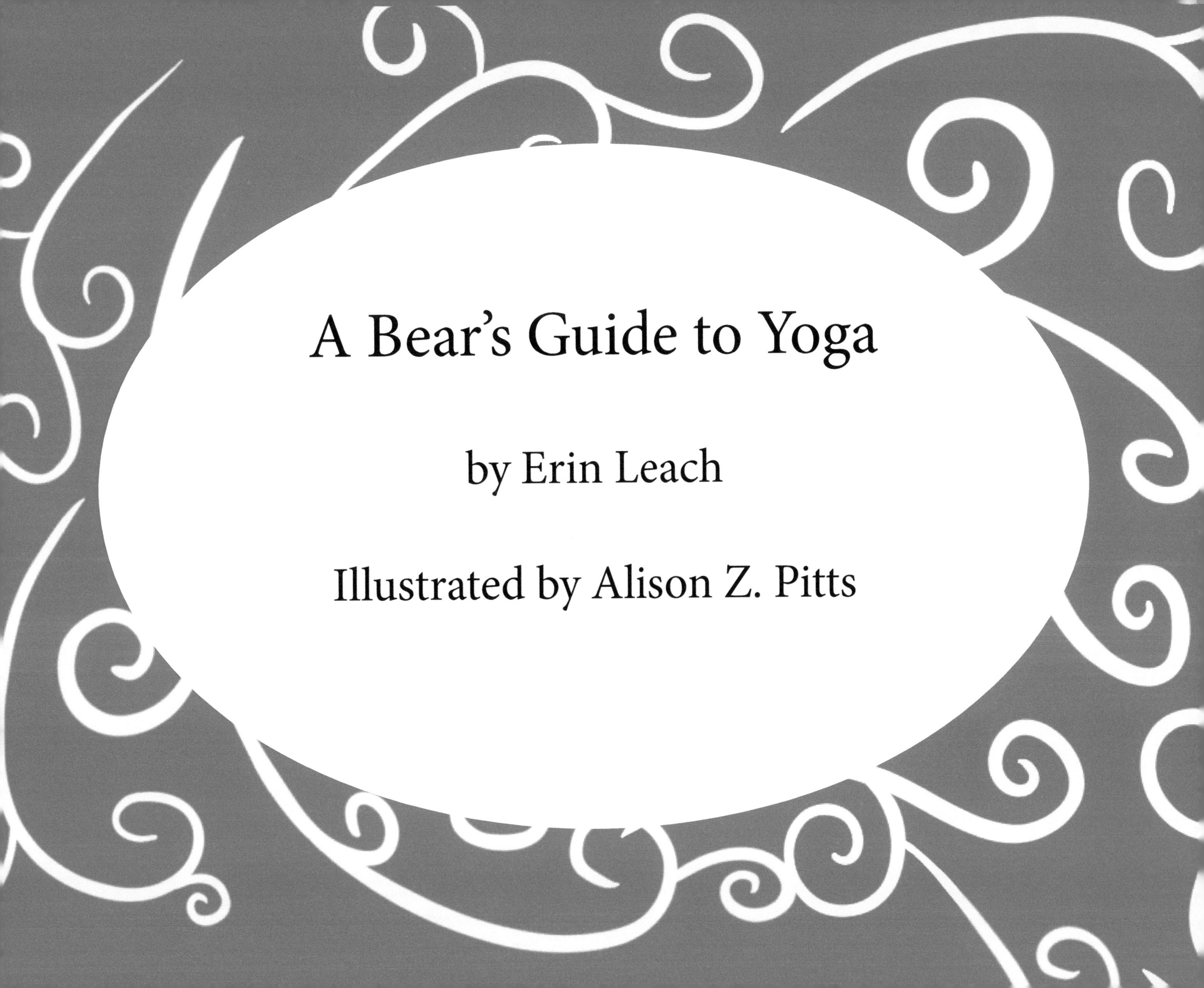

A Bear's Guide to Yoga

by Erin Leach

Illustrated by Alison Z. Pitts

Every morning, mama bears and papa bears get up
early and roll out long, flat mats.

At noontime, grownup bears pause from their work, sit or stand a little taller, and twist and stretch their stiff, furry bodies.

In the evening, aunts, uncles, cousins, brothers, sisters, and friends lie down, rest their legs on the wall, and just breathe.

What are all these bears doing day in and day out, morning, noon, and night?

They are practicing yoga! Stretching and strengthening their bear muscles, breathing fully with their bear lungs, and helping their bear minds and bodies stay healthy and well.

Anyone can practice yoga,
including you!

Try sitting up tall, closing your eyes, and taking a big breath in. Feel your belly filling up with fresh, clean air. Now let it out slowly and feel the air traveling out of your body and into the universe. You are practicing yoga!

Practicing yoga is simple and easy (most of the time). All you need to do is find a little bit of space (a chair or the floor will do), focus on breathing, and make some shapes with your body that make you
feel good.

There is no wrong way to practice yoga!

Sometimes it is hard to practice yoga. We might be feeling grumpy, tired, or just not in the mood. Or we might be feeling frustrated because a certain pose is challenging us.

These are the times when it is most important to keep practicing.

When we work hard and try our best
on our yoga mat, we do the same out
in the world.

We tell ourselves,
"I can do hard things!"

You can always ask to join a grownup in their yoga practice.
It is more fun to practice with a friend!

There are even some poses
that you can practice
together!

11

If you practice a little bit of yoga each day, you will notice
that some changes start to happen.

Your body will start to become stronger and more flexible.

Your thoughts will start to become more
clear and calm.

And you will be able to use your breath to help you work
through hard times.

This isn't magic. This is yoga helping you discover your inner superpowers! We all have them.

If everyone on Earth practiced a little bit of yoga every day, the world just might start to become a healthier, happier place.

Let that change begin with you.

Morning Yoga Sequence

Easy Seated Pose

Side Stretch
(do both sides)

Seated Open
Heart Pose

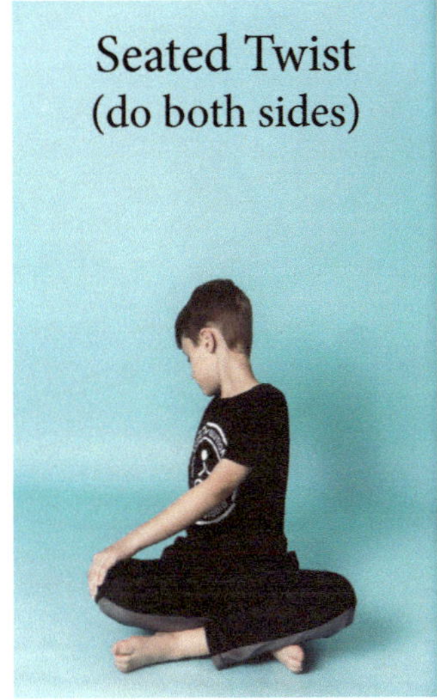

Seated Twist
(do both sides)

Downward Facing
Dog

Forward Fold

Extended
Mountain Pose

Washing Machine
Pose

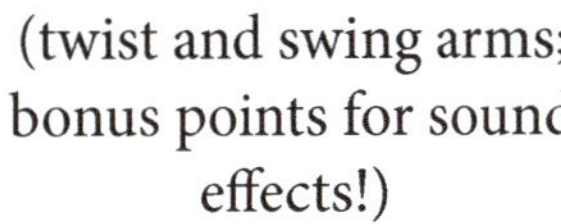

(twist and swing arms;
bonus points for sound
effects!)

Yoga Squat

Waterfall Pose

Afternoon Yoga Sequence
(Chair Yoga)

Tall Seated Pose

Extended Seated Mountain

Knee to Chest
(do both sides)

Chair Twist
(do both sides)

Chair Dog

Seated Forward Fold

Chair Figure 4
(do both sides)

Chair Savasana

Evening Yoga Sequence

Child's Pose with Hip Press

Cow Pose

Cat Pose

Seated Wide Leg Forward Fold

Butterfly Pose

Table Pose

Bridge Pose

Legs Up the Wall

Tips for Practicing Yoga at Home with Your Child

- Model the practice yourself. Children do what we DO, not what we say.

- Invite your child to practice with you, but don't make it mandatory. Offer a yoga practice, but never force a yoga practice.

- Create a special yoga spot in your home. It doesn't need to be anything fancy—a couple of inexpensive mats will do. Make it more inviting by adding yoga props, battery-operated candles, statues, crystals, or any other special artifacts.

- Schedule times to practice where they naturally fit in your day—upon waking, just before lunch, or as part of your bedtime routine.

- Keep practice times short, at least in the beginning. Three to five minutes can be plenty for little yogis!

- Find ways to practice yoga out in the world. At the park, at the bus stop, or waiting in line at the grocery store are good places to start!

- Remember that yoga is a PRACTICE! There is no end goal, and some days will be harder than others. Be gentle and forgiving with yourself (and your child).

- Keep your yoga lighthearted and FUN! Yoga does not have to be serious.

About the Author

Erin Leach began practicing yoga as a college student and immediately fell in love with the overall sense of strength and peace she felt after each practice. Yoga has been a part of her life ever since. As a former elementary school teacher and counselor, Erin has seen firsthand the benefits of yoga for children, which led her to complete her first training with ChildLight Yoga and Mindfulness for Children in 2014. Since that time, she has gone on to complete her RYT-200 certification, prenatal yoga teacher training, and 95-hour Registered Children's Yoga Teacher (RCYT) certification so that she may share the transformative power and joy of yoga with all people. She currently teaches studio classes for children and adults in Bel Air, MD and works with private clients for mindful therapy sessions.

In addition to her work in the field of yoga, Erin is a Licensed Clinical Professional Counselor (LCPC), as well as an adjunct faculty member in the graduate School of Education at Loyola University Maryland, where she developed and now teaches courses on how to incorporate yoga and mindfulness into the domain of professional school counseling.

When Erin is not teaching or practicing yoga, she enjoys reading, sewing, being outdoors (especially on the water), and spending time with her husband and two sons. You can learn more about her work at www.MamaBearYoga.com.

About the Illustrator

Alison holds a M.Ed. in Art Education from Towson University. She is an artist, art educator, and beginner yogi. When she isn't illustrating stories, working on commissions, or teaching local art classes, she enjoys working on her own yoga practice. Alison Pitts lives in Harford County, Maryland with her family.

www.ingramcontent.com/pod-product-compliance
Lightning Source LLC
Chambersburg PA
CBHW042030050726

47599CB00005B/854